Follow-the-Directions
Pocket Chart
Activities

20 Pocket Chart Activities With Templates That Guide Kids Step-by-Step to Make Cut & Paste Art Projects and Learn the Important Skill of Following Directions

by Valerie SchifferDanoff

NEW YORK • TORONTO • LONDON • AUCKLAND • SYDNEY
MEXICO CITY • NEW DELHI • HONG KONG • BUENOS AIRES

SCHOLASTIC
Teaching
Resources

Dedicated to the delight of the children I teach.

Cover design by Jason Robinson
Cover illustrations by Vincent Ceci
Cover photography by Studio 10
Interior design, illustrations, and photos by Josué Castilleja,
except page 29 by James Graham Hale
Edited by Lynn Mondello Caggiano

ISBN: 0-439-44856-5
Copyright © 2004 by Valerie SchifferDanoff.
Published by Scholastic Inc.
All rights reserved.

2 3 4 5 6 7 8 9 10   40   11 10 09 08 07 06 05 04

CONTENTS

Introduction

Following directions is an essential skill for children to develop—one that helps them become independent and effective learners. Once children are able to follow directions, they become more successful working with classmates and working on their own. As they get older, students need to be able to follow directions to complete homework and perform well on tests. In order to prepare students for these tasks—and to help them function effectively in the primary classroom—it is important to provide young children with practice in following directions.

Follow-the-Directions Pocket Chart Activities helps children learn to follow directions with twenty fun and easy pocket chart activities. Simply write the steps on sentence strips, display in a pocket chart, and invite children to follow the directions to create colorful cut-and-paste art projects. This process teaches students that they can reach objectives by dividing larger tasks into smaller steps. The activities are theme based and span the school year, making them easy to incorporate into your teaching. Projects connect to favorite themes, such as animals, holidays, and seasons, and reinforce concepts, such as shapes, colors, and numbers. You'll find an apple tree for autumn harvest, a cornucopia for Thanksgiving, a lovebug for Valentine's Day, flowers for springtime, and much more. Each lesson lists the materials needed, simple step-by-step pocket chart directions, reproducible templates, a brief introduction to the project, quick and easy variations and extension activities, and book links.

Pocket charts are a natural tool for teaching directions because each step can be written and displayed on its own sentence strip. To give children visual guidance for reading the steps, trace and cut out the templates and place them beside the appropriate steps. (For example, place a red paper flower beside the step "Trace and cut out a red flower.") The directions can also be used as the focus of a shared reading experience. The use of repetitive language helps emergent readers gain confidence as they are reading the directions. Reading aloud the directions to children gives them practice following both oral and written directions.

How to Use This Book

Look through the Table of Contents and choose a project. The projects are arranged to take you through the school year, starting with a back-to-school bus and moving through the seasons. Use the projects in the order they are presented or choose ones that connect to a particular unit of study. Feel free to adapt the activities as you see fit to meet the needs of your students and the requirements of your curriculum. The multistep directions for each project often include repetitive language and follow a basic pattern—trace and cut one or more templates from colored construction paper, glue the project together, and add details with crayons or markers. The directions can easily be adapted to meet the needs of your students. Simplify projects by leaving out steps, specifying a color instead of allowing children to choose, and so on. Extend projects by adding steps or including a writing component.

Once you have selected an activity, read through the teacher pages (pages 8–47) for ideas on introducing the project and extending the activity. The activities in this book require simple advance preparation. Gather the materials listed and photocopy the templates. It is a good idea to create oaktag templates because they are easier to trace. To save paper, have students share templates. Write the directions and project title on sturdy sentence strips (see Teaching Tips on page 7) and display in a pocket chart.

Trace and cut out the template shapes and place them beside the appropriate steps. Match the color of paper to the color specified in the directions. For example, for the bus project, trace and cut out a yellow bus and place it beside step 1. Trace and cut out two black wheels to place beside step 2, and three white windows to place beside step 3. Complete a sample project to display at the bottom of the pocket chart. The photographs on the teacher pages show how to set up each pocket chart.

To introduce and build interest in the project, use one or more of the ideas described in the Getting Started section. These might include asking discussion questions, reading aloud a picture book, or taking a class poll and charting the results. Before reading from the pocket chart, describe the project that children will make. For example, you might say, "Today, we will make party hats out of colored construction paper. We will add colored dots and ruffles to make them look more festive. When we have finished, we will store our hats in the party trunk until our New Year's celebration." Show students a completed sample project.

Direct students' attention to the pocket chart. Read aloud the directions with students. (If necessary, read aloud the directions once before having students join in.) Point to each word as you read to reinforce early literacy skills such as sound-letter correspondence. Read the numbers aloud to reinforce the concept of ordered steps. As you are reading, pause briefly after each step. Encourage students to use the visual clues presented on the pocket chart to help them read the text.

Distribute supplies and have students begin their projects. As students are working, walk around the room to check their progress. Review the steps with individual students or with the class as needed. Once children have finished, display the completed projects near the pocket chart. Have students review the steps they followed to complete the project. To extend the activity, choose one or more of the extension activities listed in the teacher pages. You might use one of the book links as a closing activity.

To give children additional practice reading directions, choose any of the following activities. These can be done in a learning center.

- Remove the sentence strips and challenge students to place them back in the pocket chart in the correct order.
- Cut apart the words in one sentence. Have children arrange them in the correct order.
- Create rebus cards for some of the words. Ask children to match the rebus pictures to the appropriate words.
- Make an additional set of directions. Cut apart the words and have children match the words to those displayed in the pocket chart.
- Remove the paper shapes from the pocket chart. Ask children to read the text and place the shapes beside the appropriate steps.

Displaying a Pocket Chart

Choose a place to display the pocket chart where children can easily see it when they are creating their projects. Children enjoy being able to walk up to a pocket chart at eye level and read the strips or manipulate the pieces. Pocket charts can be displayed on a bulletin board—secured by long, sturdy pushpins—or they can be hung from an easel with easel clips. Heavy-duty Velcro™ can also be used to hang pocket charts from walls or shelves. Pocket chart stands are available at teaching supply stores and in catalogs.

You may find that pocket charts curl inward when suspended. To alleviate this problem, place a thin dowel cut to the width of the chart in the bottom pocket, behind the sentence strip. Dowels cut to size can be purchased at hardware stores, home stores, and craft shops.

Teaching Tips

- Before beginning the activities, teach the class how to trace and cut shapes using a template. Provide a circle, square, and rectangle template for each child to trace and cut.
- Cut the templates from oaktag. Young children will have an easier time tracing sturdy shapes.
- If you would like students to create larger projects, enlarge the templates on a photocopier and provide larger construction paper.
- Label templates to provide additional practice in reading. Students can match the labels to the words in the directions, such as *flower* or *cloud*.
- Organize a work area so that all materials are easily accessible to students. In advance, cut paper and templates as indicated in the teacher pages. Store paper, templates, and any other materials in labeled baskets or small bins. Show students where everything is stored so they will be able to put materials away when finished. Designate places to store students' completed projects and works-in-progress.
- Write the directions on sturdy sentence strips using permanent marker.
- On the sentence strips, use rebus pictures in addition to or instead of words. This allows children to use visual clues to help them read the text. Write color words in the appropriate colors (as long as they are dark enough to be read easily) or place a piece of colored paper above the color word.

Storage Ideas

Once you've created sentence strips, templates, and a sample project, you'll need a place to store them when they are not in use. Consider the following storage solutions:

- Large corrugated cardboard folders allow you to store the sample art projects and templates along with the sentence strips. These folders easily tuck up against a wall or between two pieces of furniture.
- Fold a large piece of cardboard in half to make a folder; place the sentence strips inside.
- Use a butterfly clip, large paper clip, or small clamp to store sets of strips together.
- Store sentence strips in a long-stem flower box; a wallpaper box, cut along the top; or two manila folders, opened, folded lengthwise and taped together.

Resources for Pocket Chart Supplies

Pocket charts are available in a variety of sizes and colors, as are sentence strips. The typical pocket chart is 34 by 42 inches with ten pockets. Larger and smaller sizes are also available. Precut 3- by 24-inch tag-quality sentence strips are available from many sources. You might also cut your own sentence strips from pads of heavy paper. Pocket chart supplies are available from these and other retailers:

- Teaching Resource Center (1-800-833-3389)
- School Specialty (1-888-388-3224)

School Bus

Themes & Concepts

- transportation • school
- shapes • colors

Materials

- ✔ 6 sentence strips
- ✔ bus, wheel, and window templates (page 48)
- ✔ 9- by 12-inch yellow, black, and white construction paper
- ✔ pencils
- ✔ scissors
- ✔ glue
- ✔ markers or crayons

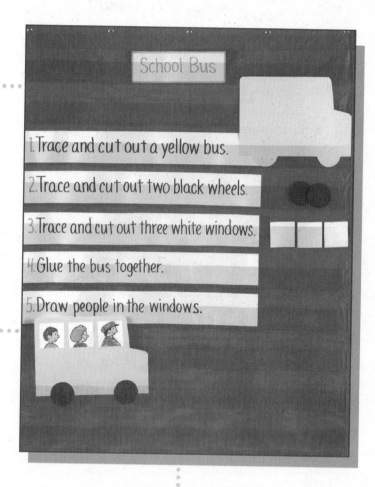

Pocket Chart Directions

School Bus

1. Trace and cut out a yellow bus.
2. Trace and cut out two black wheels.
3. Trace and cut out three white windows.
4. Glue the bus together.
5. Draw people in the windows.

Getting Started

Read aloud *This Is the Way We Go to School* by Edith Baer (Scholastic, 1992). Discuss the ways students travel to school each morning. As you introduce the pocket chart, ask children to identify the shapes and colors of the bus's windows and wheels.

Variations & Extensions

✳ Make a class chart to reflect the different ways students travel to school. On a large sheet of chart paper, draw several columns with the headings *Bus*, *Car*, *Subway*, *Walk*, and *Other*. Draw a symbol for each heading. Ask children to come up to the chart and draw an *X* in the column that represents their mode of transportation to school each day.

✳ Sing "Wheels on the Bus" together. Ask children to make up different movements for each verse.

✳ Using the bus template as a guide, make a class book about riding a bus. Give children writing prompts, such as:
    "On the bus, I saw…"
    "On the way to school…"
    "My favorite thing about riding the bus is…"

✳ To reinforce following oral directions, have children stand up holding their completed project. Then give them directions such as:
    "Drive your bus over your head."
    "Drive your bus in a circle."
    "Drive your bus from side to side."
Have children move their buses according to the oral directions. Then have them take turns giving directions to the class.

✳ Discuss the importance of drivers following directions on the road. Ask students what they notice about how directions are provided to drivers. What kinds of signs do they see? Show students drawings or photographs of different signs, such as signs for stop, yield, pedestrian crossing, and so on, and explain what each of them means. Ask students if they have ever seen a traffic officer directing traffic. What kind of directions does a traffic officer provide? How does a traffic officer communicate with drivers? Ask students to demonstrate.

Book Links

The Flying School Bus
by Seymour Reit
(Golden, 1990)

The Wheels on the Bus
by Maryann Kovalski
(Little, Brown and Company, 1987)

The Wheels on the Bus
by Paul O. Zelinsky
(Dutton Books, 1990)

My Name

Themes & Concepts

- children's names
- letter recognition
- sound-letter correspondence

Materials

- ✔ 7 sentence strips
- ✔ A to Z letter templates (pages 49–52)
- ✔ 9- by 12-inch construction paper (any colors)
- ✔ 12- by 18-inch construction paper (any colors)
- ✔ pencils
- ✔ scissors
- ✔ glue
- ✔ crayons or markers

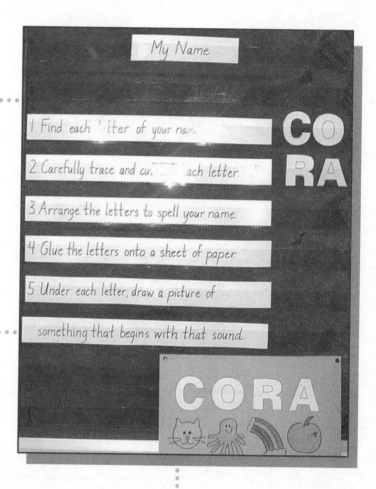

Pocket Chart Directions

My Name

1. Find each letter of your name.
2. Carefully trace and cut out each letter.
3. Arrange the letters to spell your name.
4. Glue the letters onto a sheet of paper.
5. Under each letter, draw a picture of something that begins with that sound.

Getting Started

This is a great activity to help students learn one another's names at the beginning of the year. Discuss the importance of names. Explain that names have special meanings to each person and family. Tell students that they will create a project that celebrates their name and shows the different letters and sounds in it. After reviewing letters and their sounds, say students' names aloud. Ask students to listen carefully to the different sounds in each name. Show students the sample project and brainstorm other objects that begin with each letter. Refer to alphabet books for additional practice.

Make enlarged copies of the templates on a photocopier. Divide the class into small groups. Give each group copies of the letter templates to share. Explain that for letters such as *B*, *R*, and *D*, students should draw the inside of the letter rather than cut it out. Demonstrate and offer assistance as needed.

Variations & Extensions

✳ Have students trace and cut out their initials. Change the pocket chart directions to read:
1. Find the first letter of your first name.
2. Find the first letter of your middle name.
3. Find the first letter of your last name.
4. Carefully trace and cut out each letter.
5. Glue the letters onto a sheet of paper.
6. Under each letter, draw a picture of something that begins with that sound.

✳ How many students' names begin with the letter *A*? *B*? How about *C*? As a class, chart how many names in your class begin with each letter.

✳ Make an alphabet frieze for the classroom. Invite children to find the first letter of their name. Have them draw a picture of themselves and display it under the appropriate letter. This is another way to chart how many names begin with each letter.

✳ Display the projects where students can easily see them. Tell students to find their project and then listen carefully to the directions you are about to give them. Give directions such as:
"If your name begins with *S*, clap your hands three times."
"If you have more than five letters in your name, jump on one foot."
"If you have an *E* anywhere in your name, wiggle your fingers."

Book Links

Chrysanthemum
by Kevin Henkes
(Greenwillow, 1991)

Eating the Alphabet
by Lois Ehlert
(Harcourt, 1989)

The Letters Are Lost!
by Lisa Campbell Ernst
(Viking, 1996)

Autumn Apple Tree

Themes & Concepts

- autumn • apples
- trees • counting

Materials

- ✔ 6 sentence strips
- ✔ tree and apple templates (page 53)
- ✔ 9- by 12-inch brown, green, and red construction paper
- ✔ pencils
- ✔ scissors
- ✔ glue

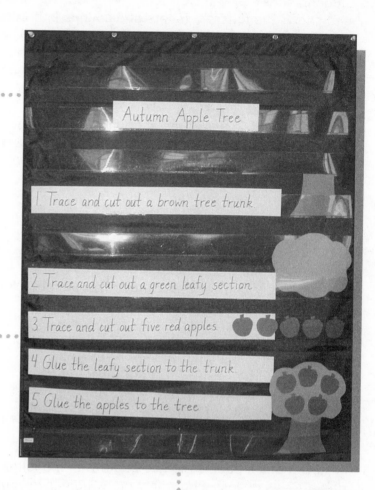

Pocket Chart Directions

Autumn Apple Tree

1. Trace and cut out a brown tree trunk.
2. Trace and cut out a green leafy section.
3. Trace and cut out five red apples.
4. Glue the leafy section to the trunk.
5. Glue the apples to the tree.

Getting Started

Read aloud *Apples* by Gail Gibbons (Holiday House, 2000) and then discuss the facts children learned about apples. Review different kinds of apples. What do they look like? How do they taste? Bring in several varieties of apples and cut them into small pieces for students to taste. Which type do they prefer? Have children vote for their favorite kind of apple and then graph the results together. (Note: Check with families first about food allergies and dietary restrictions.)

Variations & Extensions

✳ Using the apple template, trace and cut out ten apples. Create a tree using the templates, but do not glue apples onto it. Counting together with students, place five apples on the tree. Place the other five apples below the tree and count them. Are the apples on the tree equal in number to the apples below the tree? Match each apple below the tree to an apple on the tree. Ask: "Are the two groups equal?" Reinforce the concept using other manipulatives as needed. You might also use the tree and apples to review simple addition and subtraction problems.

✳ Display the completed projects on a wall or bulletin board. Ask students how they could go about counting all the apples in your classroom "orchard." Lead them to the conclusion that they could count by ones, twos, fives, or tens. Count the apples together in some of these ways.

✳ What other trees bear fruit? Using an encyclopedia or the Internet, investigate other fruit-bearing trees.

✳ Study the parts of a tree. Create a large tree from craft paper and label the different parts.

✳ To reinforce following directions and patterning skills, have students trace and cut out additional apples from both green and red construction paper. Give students a series of directions, such as:
 "Make a pattern with your apples. Start with a green apple."
 "Make a pattern with your apples. Use eight apples in all."
 "Continue this pattern with your apples: red, green, red, green."

Book Links

The Apple Pie Tree
by Zoe Hall
(Scholastic, 1996)

Apples and Pumpkins
by Anne Rockwell
(Simon & Schuster, 1989)

How Do Apples Grow?
by Betsy Maestro
(HarperCollins, 1992)

The Seasons of Arnold's Apple Tree
by Gail Gibbons
(Harcourt, 1984)

Jack-o'-Lantern

Themes & Concepts

- fruits and vegetables
- harvest
- expressions and emotions

Materials

- ✔ 6 sentence strips
- ✔ jack-o'-lantern templates (pages 54–55)
- ✔ 9- by 12-inch orange, green, and black construction paper
- ✔ pencils
- ✔ scissors
- ✔ glue

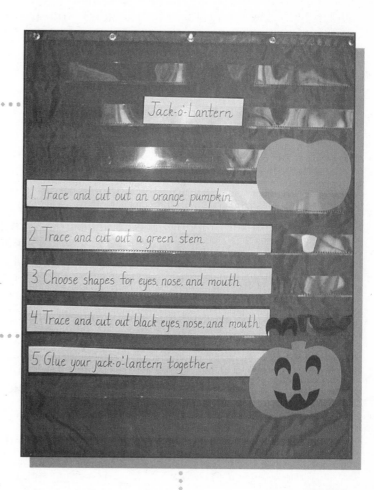

Pocket Chart Directions

Jack-o'-Lantern

1. Trace and cut out an orange pumpkin.
2. Trace and cut out a green stem.
3. Choose shapes for eyes, nose, and mouth.
4. Trace and cut out black eyes, nose, and mouth.
5. Glue your jack-o'-lantern together.

Getting Started

Read aloud *How Are You Peeling?* by Saxton Freymann (Arthur A. Levine, 1999). Discuss the emotions that are portrayed on the different fruits and vegetables. Have children guess what mood each facial expression is conveying. Ask children to talk about and demonstrate how facial expressions can convey emotions. Explain that children will create a paper jack-o'-lantern and ask them to think about what expression they would like their pumpkin to have. Scary? Surprised? Happy? How will they draw the eyes, nose, and mouth to show this particular expression?

Variations & Extensions

✳ Teach children the following song about pumpkin carving (to the tune of "The Itsy-Bitsy Spider"):

First you take a pumpkin, big and round and fat.
Then you cut the top off—that will make the hat.
Then you hollow out the nose and mouth and eyes.
And give it to children for a Halloween surprise!

✳ For younger children, provide crayons and markers. Have children draw facial features on their jack-o'-lanterns.

✳ Cut the top off a real pumpkin and allow students to take turns scooping out the pulp and seeds. Ask students if a pumpkin is a fruit or a vegetable. How do they know? Explain that a pumpkin is a fruit because it has seeds. What other fruits can children name? They might say grapes, pears, green peppers, tomatoes, and so on. Make a list together. Then ask students to name as many vegetables as they can (celery, potato, radish, and so on). If students are unsure if something is a vegetable, ask if it has seeds.

✳ Hold a real pumpkin-carving experience in your classroom! Send a letter home in advance inviting parents to volunteer and provide pumpkins for the event. Have each parent volunteer supervise a small group of students. Explain that they will work together to decide what kind of expression their jack-o'-lantern will have. Students will draw the facial features and parents will do the actual cutting. Children can help scoop out the pulp and seeds. Have each group give their jack-o'-lantern a name and introduce it to the class.

Book Links

Halloween Cats
by Jean Marzollo
(Scholastic, 1992)

The Littlest Pumpkin
by R. A. Herman
(Cartwheel, 2001)

Too Many Pumpkins
by Linda White
(Holiday House, 1996)

Vegetables, Vegetables!
by Fay Robinson
(Children's Press, 1994)

Cornucopia

Themes & Concepts

- **Thanksgiving** • **harvest**
- **fruits and vegetables**
- **colors**

Materials

✔ 8 sentence strips
✔ cornucopia and fruit templates (pages 56–57)
✔ 9- by 12-inch brown, orange, red, green, and purple construction paper
✔ pencils
✔ scissors
✔ glue
✔ markers or crayons

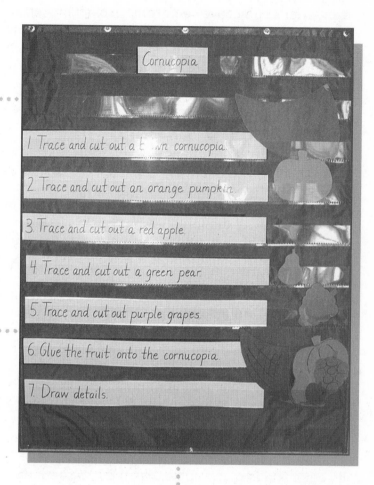

Pocket Chart Directions

Cornucopia

1. **Trace and cut out a brown cornucopia.**
2. **Trace and cut out an orange pumpkin.**
3. **Trace and cut out a red apple.**
4. **Trace and cut out a green pear.**
5. **Trace and cut out purple grapes.**
6. **Glue the fruit onto the cornucopia.**
7. **Draw details.**

Follow-the-Directions Pocket Chart Activities Scholastic Teaching Resources

Getting Started

Determine whether students are familiar with a cornucopia, or "horn of plenty." Explain that these are two names for the same item—a large horn-shaped basket that holds a variety of fruits and vegetables. Tell students that these are often seen around Thanksgiving because the fruits and vegetables inside the cornucopia traditionally represent the harvest. Using a picture or a real cornucopia, review the names of different fruits and vegetables.

Variations & Extensions

✳ Invite students to choose which kinds of fruits and vegetables they will add to their cornucopia. Create additional templates for them to choose from, or have them draw and then cut out their own fruits and vegetables. Adjust the directions as needed.

✳ Make a fruit salad using apples, grapes, and pears; enjoy at snack time as a class. Which fruit does your class like best? Take a class survey and graph the results. (Note: Check with families first about food allergies or other dietary restrictions.)

✳ As a class, make an apple pie, apple turnovers, or applesauce. (Note: Check with families first about food allergies or other dietary restrictions.) Write the recipe on chart paper and draw rebus pictures to guide children. Following a recipe is a great way to reinforce the concept of following directions. Discuss the importance of following a recipe carefully. What happens if you add the wrong ingredients? Or the wrong amounts?

✳ Discuss which fruits and vegetables are harvested in different seasons. Add pictures of each to the class calendar in the appropriate season.

✳ Make an alphabet frieze of foods that remind students of autumn and Thanksgiving. Write the letters *A* to *Z* on chart paper. Brainstorm together a food that begins with each letter. For some letters, you'll need to be creative (for example, *X* could be extra yummy pie). Fold sheets of 9- by 12-inch white construction paper in half and then cut along the fold. Write an uppercase and lowercase letter on each. Give each student a letter card. Have students draw and color an illustration of the food for that letter. Add a label and display at children's eye level.

Book Links

Apple Picking Time
by Michele Slawson
(Crown, 1994)

Harvest Year
by Cris Peterson
(Boyds Mills, 1996)

Picking Apples
& Pumpkins
by Amy and Richard Hutchings
(Scholastic, 1994)

Thanksgiving
by Laura Alden
(Children's Press, 1993)

I Spy a Pizza Pie

Themes & Concepts

- shapes • basic fractions
- counting • food

Materials

- ✔ 5 sentence strips
- ✔ large circle, medium circle, and diamond templates (page 58)
- ✔ 9- by 12-inch light brown, red, and yellow construction paper
- ✔ pencils
- ✔ scissors
- ✔ glue

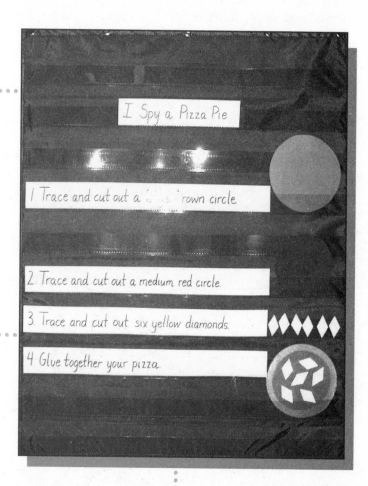

Pocket Chart Directions

I Spy a Pizza Pie

1. Trace and cut out a large brown circle.
2. Trace and cut out a medium red circle.
3. Trace and cut out six yellow diamonds.
4. Glue your pizza together.

Getting Started

Hold up a paper circle and ask children to think of foods that have the same shape. When pizza is named, ask how pizza is made. Discuss the ingredients that are used to make a pizza, such as cheese and tomatoes. Use a K-W-L chart (What I Know, What I Want to Know, What I Learned) to record what students know and what they want to know about pizza. Read aloud *Pizza Pat* by Rita Golden Gelman (Random House, 1999). Add to the K-W-L chart the information students learned.

Make two copies of the template page for each student. Show them how to cut around the large circle on one sheet and around the medium circle on the other.

Variations & Extensions

* Add different shapes to the project. Replace some of the diamonds with small circles, squares, triangles, and so on. Adjust the directions as needed.

* Have children use the large circle template to trace and cut out a circle. Then instruct them to fold the circle in half and cut along the fold. Next, show them how to fold again and cut the two halves to make four quarters. Finally, have them glue the pieces together to form a "pie" on a large sheet of paper. Use these pies as a starting place to talk about basic fractions. Ask: "How many pieces are in half a pie? How many pieces are in a whole pie?"

* Use pita bread or another round bread to make a pizza snack for your class. Or visit a local pizzeria to see how real pizza is made! (Note: Check with families first about food allergies or dietary restrictions.)

* Invite students to use descriptive language to write pizza poems. Ask each student to add a line to the poem. For example:
    Pizza is...
    gooey,
    cheesy,
    yummy,
    good to eat!

* To reinforce following directions, give students manipulatives to use with their completed projects. Provide oral directions, such as:
    "Place one chip on your pizza."
    "Place a chip under your pizza."
    "Balance your pizza on your head!"

Book Links

Little Nino's Pizzeria
by Karen Barbour
(Harcourt, 1987)

Pete's a Pizza
by William Steig
(HarperCollins, 1998)

Make Your Own Sundae

Themes & Concepts

• colors • food • sequencing

Materials

✔ 7 sentence strips
✔ bowl, ice cream, hot fudge, whipped cream, and cherry templates (page 59)
✔ 9- by 12-inch purple, pink, brown, white, and red construction paper
✔ pencils
✔ scissors
✔ glue

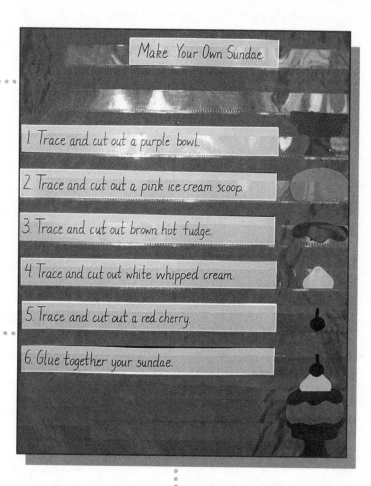

Make Your Own Sundae

1. Trace and cut out a purple bowl.
2. Trace and cut out a pink ice cream scoop.
3. Trace and cut out brown hot fudge.
4. Trace and cut out white whipped cream.
5. Trace and cut out a red cherry.
6. Glue together your sundae.

Pocket Chart Directions

Make Your Own Sundae

1. Trace and cut out a purple bowl.
2. Trace and cut out a pink ice cream scoop.
3. Trace and cut out brown hot fudge.
4. Trace and cut out white whipped cream.
5. Trace and cut out a red cherry.
6. Glue your sundae together.

Follow-the-Directions Pocket Chart Activities Scholastic Teaching Resources

Getting Started

I scream, you scream...who loves ice cream? Ask students to name their favorite ice cream flavors. Then ask: "If you could invent a flavor, what would it be?" Ask if anyone has seen an ice cream sundae being made. Discuss the steps in making a sundae—what happens first, second, and so on. As students describe the steps, write them on chart paper. Explain that these are the directions to making an ice cream sundae. Why is it important to follow the directions in order? Ask students to speculate— what would the sundae look like if you mixed up the order of the steps?

Variations & Extensions

✻ Allow students to choose their own colors for the bowl, ice cream scoop, and sauce. Change the first three steps in the pocket chart directions as follows:
  1. Trace and cut out a bowl (any color).
  2. Trace and cut out an ice cream scoop (any color).
  3. Trace and cut out a sauce topping (any color).

✻ Have students create tall paper sundaes with three or more scoops of ice cream. Provide additional colors of paper. Change the directions for the second step as follows. Specify the number of scoops students should include.
  2. Trace and cut out three ice cream scoops (any colors).

✻ Take a poll—What is the most popular flavor in the class? In the grade? In the school? Use the paper ice cream scoops to chart the results.

✻ Make real ice cream sundaes for a special snack. Have students follow the directions listed on chart paper. (Note: Check with families first about food allergies or other dietary restrictions. Soymilk and rice milk-based ice cream products can be used if necessary.)

✻ Ask students what other sets of directions need to be followed in a particular order. Baking a cake? Brushing teeth? Have children use the words *first*, *next*, *then*, and *last* as they describe the steps to the class. Write the directions on chart paper and then edit them together.

Book Links

Cone Kong: The Scary Ice Cream Giant by Daniel Manus Pinkwater (Cartwheel, 2002)

Ice Cream Larry by Daniel Manus Pinkwater (Marshall Cavendish, 1999)

I Like Ice Cream by Robin Pickering (Children's Press, 2000)

We All Scream for Ice Cream! The Scoop on America's Favorite Dessert by Lee Wardlaw (Avon, 2000)

Party Time!

Themes & Concepts

- **New Year's celebrations**
- **birthdays • shapes • colors**

Materials

✔ 9 sentence strips
✔ triangle, circle, and ruffle templates (page 60)
✔ 9- by 12-inch colored construction paper (at least four different colors)
✔ pencils
✔ scissors
✔ glue
✔ markers or crayons

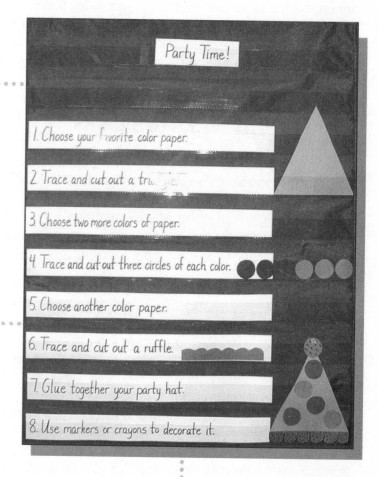

Pocket Chart Directions

Party Time!

1. Choose your favorite color paper.
2. Trace and cut out a triangle.
3. Chose two more colors of paper.
4. Trace and cut out three circles of each color.
5. Choose another color paper.
6. Trace and cut out a ruffle.
7. Glue your party hat together.
8. Use markers or crayons to decorate it.

Getting Started

Bring in party hats, either bought or made. Ask children if they have ever worn a party hat. What was the occasion? Together, brainstorm occasions that might include party hats or other party favors. Explain that children are going to follow instructions to make their own party hats. Draw a triangle and discuss its properties. Then draw a circle and discuss its properties. Ask, "How is a circle different from a triangle?" Guide student responses as needed.

Variations & Extensions

✳ To simplify this project, specify the colors you would like students to use. Modify the steps as follows:
1. Trace and cut out a blue triangle.
2. Trace and cut out three red circles.
3. Trace and cut out three yellow circles.
4. Trace and cut out a green ruffle.
5. Glue your party hat together.
6. Use markers or crayons to decorate it.

✳ Examine other shapes together. How are the shapes similar, and how are they different? Ask students what shapes they see in the classroom. On chart paper, draw a shape and write its name. As a class, brainstorm objects that are this shape. The objects might be found in the classroom or beyond.

✳ Enlarge the templates on a photocopier and make one large hat for each month. Display the hats as a birthday chart. Write each child's birthday on a paper circle and glue it to the appropriate month. Display all the hats and ask children questions such as: "Which month has the most birthdays? Which month has the least? Does every month have at least one birthday?"

✳ Read about and discuss different New Year's celebrations (see Book Links). Talk about their similarities and differences. Have students draw a picture of something they learned about one of the celebrations and then write or dictate a sentence about it.

✳ Discuss different games that are played at parties, such as pin the tail on the donkey. Choose a game that students are familiar with and work together to write simple directions for the game. Discuss the importance of following directions in a game.

Book Links

Birthdays! Celebrating Life Around the World
by Eve B. Feldman
(Troll, 1995)

Lion Dancer: Ernie Wan's Chinese New Year
by Kate Waters
(Scholastic, 1990)

Tet: The New Year
by Kim-Lan Tran
(Aladdin, 1993)

When a Line Bends... A Shape Begins
by Rhonda Gowler Greene
(Houghton Mifflin, 1997)

The World's Birthday: A Rosh Hashanah Story
by Barbara Diamond Goldin (Harcourt, 1990)

Warm Winter Mittens

Themes & Concepts

- weather • winter • snow
- seasons • clothing

Materials

- ✔ 5 sentence strips
- ✔ mitten and snowman templates (page 61)
- ✔ 9- by 12-inch white and red construction paper
- ✔ pencils
- ✔ scissors
- ✔ glue
- ✔ markers or crayons

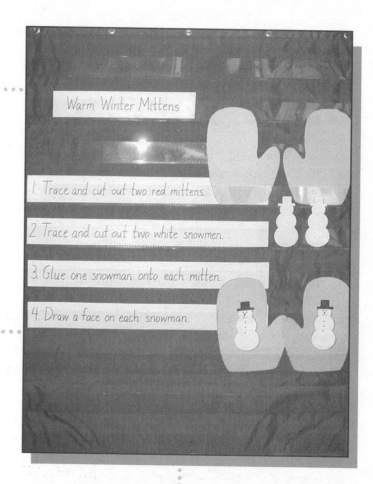

Pocket Chart Directions

Warm Winter Mittens

1. Trace and cut out two red mittens.
2. Trace and cut out two white snowmen.
3. Glue one snowman onto each mitten.
4. Draw details on each snowman.

Getting Started

Talk about the special kinds of clothing you need to keep warm in the winter. Explain how mittens keep your hands warm. Ask, "Why might children wear mittens when building snowmen?" Read one of the snowy stories (see Book Links) to build students' interest.

Show students how to trace and cut out two mittens, and then turn one over to create mittens for left and right hands.

Variations & Extensions

✳ Explain to students that mittens come in pairs. Then discuss what it means when something is part of a pair. Ask students to name other things that come in pairs, such as socks, shoes, earrings, and so on. Ask students to guess why we refer to scissors and pants as a pair (a pair of scissors and a pair of pants).

✳ If students have never seen or felt snow, use ice cubes to simulate the experience. Have students feel the ice while wearing mittens. Have them remove the mittens and quickly feel the ice again. What is the difference? Why do they think people in cold-weather climates wear mittens in the winter? Make a list of other articles of clothing that people wear in cold-weather climates. Discuss ways that lifestyle is affected by climate.

✳ Allow students to decorate their mittens with other craft items, such as sequins or glitter. Have students write haiku or another type of poem about winter. Hang the decorated mittens with the poems on a bulletin board or a clothesline to create a wintertime display.

✳ Create a class book using the mitten template. Have students dictate or write about a favorite wintertime activity on their mitten-shaped page and then draw an illustration to match the text. Add a cover and bind together with yarn.

✳ As a class, write the directions for building a snowman on chart paper. Then have students use different colors of modeling compound to follow the directions and create their own miniature snowmen.

✳ Explain that alliteration is when writers use the same sound several times in a row. Have students write or dictate alliterative sentences about winter topics, such as mittens, snowmen, snow, frost, and so on.

Book Links

The Mitten
by Jan Brett
(Putnam, 1989)

Once Upon Ice: And Other Frozen Poems
selected by Jane Yolen
(Boyds Mills, 1997)

Sadie and the Snowman
by Allen Morgan
(Scholastic, 1987)

Snowballs
by Lois Ehlert
(Harcourt, 1996)

Snow Day!
by Barbara M. Joosse
(Clarion, 1995)

Hooray for 100!

Themes & Concepts

- 100th Day of School
- counting • skip counting
- numeral recognition

Materials

- ✔ 6 sentence strips
- ✔ numeral templates for 0 and 1 (page 62)
- ✔ 9- by 12-inch construction paper (any colors)
- ✔ 12- by 18-inch light-colored construction paper
- ✔ pencils
- ✔ scissors
- ✔ glue
- ✔ markers or crayons

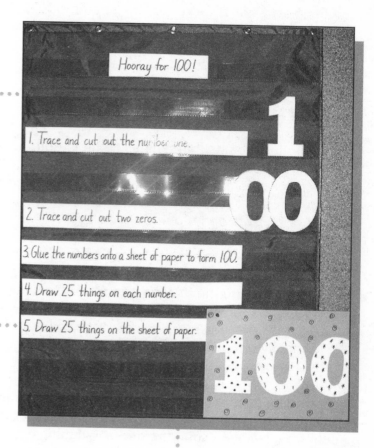

Pocket Chart Directions

Hooray for 100!

1. Trace and cut out the number one.
2. Trace and cut out two zeros.
3. Glue the numbers onto a sheet of paper to form 100.
4. Draw 25 things on each number.
5. Draw 25 things on the sheet of paper.

☀ Getting Started ☀

Begin by counting to 25. As you count, place a penny or other manipulative in a jar, one penny for each number. Count four groups of 25 in all so that the jar holds 100 pennies. Ask students to predict how many pennies are in the jar. As a class, empty the jar and count the pennies, without grouping. Explain that 100 is the same as four groups of 25.

When students reach steps 4 and 5, discuss different strategies for drawing 100 things. Instruct them to keep their drawings very simple so they are easy to draw, such as dots, X's, or small squiggles. Talk about different ways to keep track of how many things they have drawn. They might draw each group of 25 as two sets of 10 and one set of 5.

☀ Variations & Extensions ☀

✳ Have students use small stickers or stamps to decorate the numbers instead of drawing 100 items.

✳ Talk about all the ways to count to 100—by twos, fives, tens, and so on. Divide students into groups and give each group 100 small objects, such as dried beans. Have each group practice counting the objects in the different ways you discussed.

✳ Create 100th Day of School posters. Instruct students to count 100 small items, such as pieces of cereal, pieces of paper, dried beans, and so on. Then have them glue the items onto a sturdy sheet of paper. You might have them group the items on the paper into sets of 5, 10, or 20. Celebrate the 100th day of school by displaying these posters in your classroom.

✳ Reinforce counting to 100 and following directions by creating ten stations around the classroom. At each station, write a set of directions that involves doing ten tasks—do ten jumping jacks, touch your toes ten times, write ten letters or words, and so on. Add rebus pictures to help students follow the directions. Divide the class into small groups and have groups rotate from station to station to complete each of the tasks. When finished, ask students how many things they did in all.

Book Links

100th Day Worries
by Margery Cuyler
(Simon & Schuster, 2000)

Emily's First 100 Days of School
by Rosemary Wells
(Hyperion, 2000)

From One to One Hundred
by Teri Sloat
(Dutton, 1991)

Miss Bindergarten Celebrates the 100th Day of Kindergarten
by Joseph Slate
(Dutton, 1998)

One Hundred Is a Family
by Pam Muñoz Ryan
(Hyperion, 1996)

Lovable Lovebug

Themes & Concepts

- Valentine's Day • friendship
- insects • sizes

Materials

- ✔ 9 sentence strips
- ✔ small, medium, and large heart templates (page 63)
- ✔ 9- by 12-inch red and pink construction paper
- ✔ red construction paper strips (1- by 6-inch and 1- by 8-inch)
- ✔ pencils
- ✔ scissors
- ✔ glue
- ✔ markers or crayons

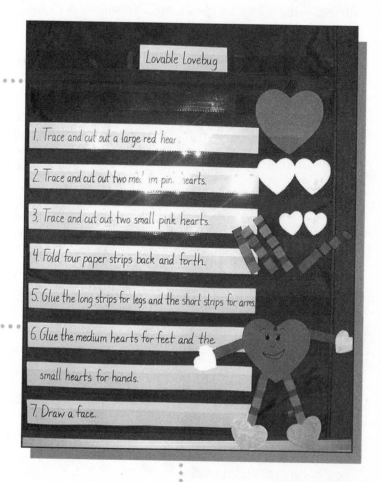

Pocket Chart Directions

Lovable Lovebug

1. Trace and cut out a large red heart.
2. Trace and cut out two medium pink hearts.
3. Trace and cut out two small pink hearts.
4. Fold four paper strips back and forth.
5. Glue the long strips for legs and the short strips for arms.
6. Glue the medium hearts for feet and the small hearts for hands.
7. Draw a face.

Follow-the-Directions Pocket Chart Activities Scholastic Teaching Resources

✣ Getting Started ✣

Describe typical Valentine's Day traditions. Tell students that on this holiday, we often send cards to let others know that they are special to us and that we are thinking of them. Tell students that they will make a lovebug for Valentine's Day. Explain that their lovebug can give a little "nip" to remind them to show their appreciation for a friend or family member. Give each student a copy of the template page along with two long paper rectangles and two short paper rectangles (see Materials).

For step 4, demonstrate how to fold the strips back and forth accordion-style.

 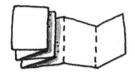

✣ Variations & Extensions ✣

✳ In advance, prepare the paper strips as a class. Give students templates in two sizes to trace and cut out the strips. Then show them how to accordion-fold the strips. Modify the pocket chart instructions as follows:
1. Trace and cut out a large red heart.
2. Trace and cut out two medium pink hearts.
3. Trace and cut out two small pink hearts.
4. Glue the long strips for legs and the short strips for arms.
5. Glue the medium hearts for feet and the small hearts for hands.
6. Draw a face.

✳ Instead of drawing eyes, give students movable eyes to glue onto their lovebugs. You might also give them black pipe cleaners to add antennae.

✳ Attach string or yarn to the back of each lovebug. Display the finished lovebugs throughout the classroom or hallway so that they appear to be flying.

✳ Invite children to draw and cut out their own lovebugs. Add these to a bulletin board display along with large paper flowers to create a "garden of love."

✳ Ask students if a lovebug is a real insect. How do they know? Use this project to introduce a unit on insects.

Book Links

Counting Kisses
by Karen Katz
(Margaret K. McElderry, 2001)

Little Mouse's Big Valentine
by Thatcher Hurd
(Harper, 1990)

The Valentine Bears
by Eve Bunting
(Clarion, 1984)

Valentine's Day
by Gail Gibbons
(Holiday House, 1986)

In Like a Lion

Themes & Concepts

- spring • seasons
- weather • lions
- comparing and contrasting

Materials

✔ 7 sentence strips
✔ lion face, body, tail, and mane templates (pages 64–65)
✔ 9- by 12-inch brown and yellow construction paper
✔ pencil
✔ scissors
✔ glue
✔ markers or crayons

In Like a Lion
1. Trace and cut out a brown face.
2. Trace and cut out a brown body.
3. Trace and cut out a brown tail.
4. Trace and cut out a yellow mane.
5. Glue the lion together.
6. Draw a face.

Pocket Chart Directions

In Like a Lion

1. Trace and cut out a brown face.
2. Trace and cut out a brown body.
3. Trace and cut out a brown tail.
4. Trace and cut out a yellow mane.
5. Glue the lion together.
6. Draw a face.

Getting Started

As a class, list the traits of a lion (fierce and wild). Next, list the characteristics of a lamb (calm and gentle). Introduce the old adage, "March comes in like a lion and goes out like a lamb." Explain that March is the month when winter turns into spring. Ask students to think about the saying and discuss what it means. Talk about the early spring weather. How is early spring different from winter? How is it the same? Ask students to speculate which type of weather the lion represents—winter or spring? What about the lamb? Take a class vote.

Variations & Extensions

* If you have space in your classroom, display this pocket chart activity beside the lamb activity that follows (pages 32–33). You might have half the class make one project and half the class make the other, or have children choose which one they would like to create.

* Keep track of the March weather to see how many days are mild and how many days are cold and blustery. Keep a tally of days that are "like a lion" and days that are "like a lamb." Draw two columns on chart paper and add a simple illustration of a lion at the top of one and a lamb at the top of the other. Show children how to make tally marks in each column. Throughout the month, ask children, "Which has more days, the lion or the lamb? Which do you think will have more days at the end of the month?" At the end of the month, count the tally marks and see whose predictions were accurate.

* If you live in a temperate climate, use the Internet to keep track of the weather in a place that experiences more dramatic seasonal changes.

* Choose a place that has very different weather from your area. Using the Internet, find out the weather of this place every day and compare it to your own. Chart the weather in each place and note similarities and differences.

* Invite students to write or dictate descriptions of stormy weather.

Book Links

Dandelion
by Don Freeman
(Viking, 1964)

Horrible Hair
by Gerald Rose
(Andersen, 2001)

*In for Winter,
Out for Spring*
by Arnold Adoff
(Harcourt, 1991)

One Windy Wednesday
by Phyllis Root
(Candlewick, 1997)

The Wind Blew
by Pat Hutchins
(Atheneum, 1974)

Out Like a Lamb

Themes & Concepts

- spring • seasons
- lambs • weather
- comparing and contrasting

Materials

- ✔ 7 sentence strips
- ✔ lamb body, head, fleece, and leg templates (pages 66–67)
- ✔ 9- by 12-inch white, pink, and black construction paper
- ✔ pencils
- ✔ scissors
- ✔ glue
- ✔ markers or crayons

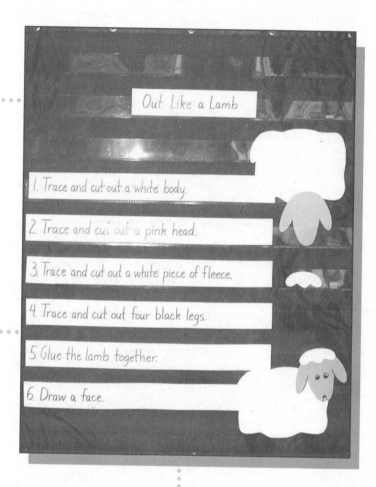

Out Like a Lamb

1. Trace and cut out a white body.
2. Trace and cut out a pink head.
3. Trace and cut out a white piece of fleece.
4. Trace and cut out four black legs.
5. Glue the lamb together.
6. Draw a face.

Pocket Chart Directions

Out Like a Lamb

1. Trace and cut out a white body.
2. Trace and cut out a pink head.
3. Trace and cut out a white piece of fleece.
4. Trace and cut out four black legs.
5. Glue the lamb together.
6. Draw a face.

Getting Started

If using this project as a follow-up to "In Like a Lion," (pages 30–31), review the expression "March comes in like a lion and goes out like a lamb." Ask students to recall the characteristics of a lion and a lamb and to explain how these descriptions can apply to the different kinds of weather in the month of March.

Variations & Extensions

✻ Explain that fleece is the lamb's soft woolly coat. It refers to the soft wool all over their bodies and on their heads, as in step 3. As an added step, children can glue cotton balls onto their lambs' coats.

✻ Pair this project with "In Like a Lion" (pages 30–31) and display the two projects side by side. See Variations and Extensions on page 31 for activities to compare and contrast the two kinds of weather in March.

✻ Challenge students to think of other kinds of weather that remind them of animals. Or have them change the expression about March so that it compares the weather to two different animals—for example, "March comes in like a bear and goes out like a butterfly."

✻ Ask students in what months other seasons change. What kind of weather marks the end of autumn and the beginning of winter? When does this take place in your area? How about the end of summer and the beginning of fall? Have students write or dictate descriptions of each of these changes in season.

✻ Use the lion and lamb templates to create collaborative shape books. Assemble each animal; then trace and cut out a card-stock template. Have children trace the template, cut out a page, and either write or dictate a sentence or poem about the end of winter (lion book) and the beginning of spring (lamb book). Invite them to illustrate their pages. Use the completed lamb or lion for the cover and bind the pages together.

✻ Invite students to write or dictate descriptions of the soft rains and gentle weather generally associated with spring.

Book Links

Hopper Hunts for Spring
by Marcus Pfister
(North-South, 1995)

It's Spring!
by Linda Glaser
(Millbrook, 2002)

Mud Flat Spring
by James Stevenson
(Greenwillow, 1999)

Strudwick: A Sheep in Wolf's Clothing
by Robert Kraus
(Viking, 1995)

April Showers Mobile

Themes & Concepts

- colors • seasons • weather
- plants • flowers
- water cycle

Materials

✔ 8 sentence strips
✔ cloud, raindrop, flower, and stem templates (pages 68–69)
✔ 9- by 12-inch white, blue, red, and green construction paper
✔ 1- by 10-inch strips of white construction paper
✔ pencils
✔ scissors
✔ glue

Pocket Chart Directions

April Showers Mobile

1. **Trace and cut out a white cloud.**
2. **Trace and cut out nine blue raindrops.**
3. **Trace and cut out three red flowers.**
4. **Trace and cut out three green stems.**
5. **Glue three white strips to the cloud.**
6. **Glue the raindrops to the strips.**
7. **Glue a flower and stem to the bottom of each strip.**

Follow-the-Directions Pocket Chart Activities Scholastic Teaching Resources

Getting Started

Talk about spring as a time of growth and renewal. Discuss the changes that typically signal the arrival of spring. Have students noticed such changes in your area? Have they seen flowers sprouting? Examine different plant seeds. Explain how these seeds will grow into plants when planted in soil and fortified with water and light. Can students guess how seeds obtain water and light?

Give each student three white strips along with the templates (see Materials).

Variations & Extensions

* Add a touch of spring to your classroom. Attach string or yarn to the back of each project and hang from the ceiling.

* Fill small paper cups with soil. Plant seeds and water regularly. Have students measure and chart the seedling growth every few days. As an alternative, place beans and a moist paper towel in a resealable plastic bag. Keep the towel moist. The bean should begin to sprout within a few days.

* If possible, arrange a class tour of a local farm or nursery.

* Discuss different kinds of clouds:
    cirrus: wispy, thin clouds
    cumulus: large, fluffy clouds
    stratus: long layers of clouds
Each day, have students take part in a "cloud watch." Keep a record of the types of clouds that they see.

* Write a collaborative poem about rain that includes the senses. How does rain sound and feel? How does a rainy day look and smell?

* Teach students about the water cycle. Explain that the sun heats the ocean and causes some of its water to evaporate. Air currents lift the water vapor so that it rises off the ocean. The water vapor eventually reaches cooler air and condenses into small water droplets or ice crystals. These water droplets come together to form larger water droplets. When they become heavy enough, they fall from the clouds to the ground as rain or snow (precipitation). Three-fourths of precipitation returns to the ocean and the cycle repeats. The ground absorbs some precipitation, which is then taken in by plants. Plants also give off water vapor through their leaves.

Book Links

From Seed to Plant
by Gail Gibbons
(Holiday House, 1991)

Planting a Rainbow
by Lois Ehlert
(Harcourt, 1988)

The Tiny Seed
by Eric Carle
(Simon & Schuster, 1987)

Water Dance
by Thomas Locker
(Harcourt, 1997)

My Pet Puppy

- dogs • pets • pet care

Materials

- ✔ 8 sentence strips
- ✔ puppy body, head, and bowl templates (pages 70–71)
- ✔ 9- by 12-inch brown and yellow construction paper
- ✔ 12- by 18-inch red construction paper
- ✔ pencils
- ✔ scissors
- ✔ glue
- ✔ markers or crayons

Pocket Chart Directions

My Pet Puppy

1. Trace and cut out a brown body.
2. Trace and cut out a brown head.
3. Glue the puppy together on red paper.
4. Draw a face.
5. Trace and cut out a yellow bowl.
6. Glue the bowl next to the puppy.
7. Write the puppy's name on the bowl.

Getting Started

This project is a nice way to celebrate Be Kind to Animals Week, during the first week of May. To begin, ask students if they have a pet or would like to have a pet. What kinds of pets do they have or would they like to have? What do they like about pets? Allow students to share a few pet stories. Do different kinds of pets have similar characteristics? Explain to students that they will follow directions to make a pet out of paper. Distribute the templates. Ask children to guess what kind of pet they will be making. How do they know?

Variations & Extensions

✳ For the last step, have younger students dictate instead of write the name of their puppy.

✳ To simplify the directions, leave out the bowl. To extend the directions, have students use white or black paper to add spots to their puppy. Add instructions to the pocket chart :
   5. Cut out spots from white or black paper.
   6. Glue the spots onto your puppy.
(Change the numbers of steps 5 to 7 accordingly.)

✳ Have students write or dictate a story about an adventure involving their new pet. Explain that the main character can be the student, the puppy, or another character. Invite students to illustrate a scene from their stories. Display the stories and illustrations beside students' projects.

✳ Invite a veterinarian or representative from a local animal welfare group to talk to your class about pet care. As a follow-up activity, have students create posters to show what they learned. Create a hallway display about pet care.

✳ To reinforce following directions, play Simon Says with an animal twist. This works best in a large open space. Give students a series of oral directions such as:
   "Simon says walk like an elephant to the front of the room."
   "Simon says swing your trunk from side to side."
   "Balance on one foot like a flamingo."
Have students take turns being the leader.

Book Links

Dogs
by Gail Gibbons
(Holiday House, 1997)

Henry and Mudge:
The First Book
by Cynthia Rylant
(Aladdin, 1990)

"Let's Get a Pup!"
Said Kate
by Bob Graham
(Candlewick, 2001)

Lucy Comes to Stay
by Rosemary Wells
(Dial, 1994)

The Stray Dog
by Marc Simont
(HarperCollins, 2001)

My Pet Cat

Themes & Concepts

- domestic and wild cats
- pets • pet care
- comparing and contrasting

Materials

- ✔ 8 sentence strips
- ✔ cat body, head, and bowl templates (pages 72–73)
- ✔ 9- by 12-inch gray and orange construction paper
- ✔ 12- by 18-inch blue construction paper
- ✔ pencils
- ✔ scissors
- ✔ glue
- ✔ markers or crayons

Pocket Chart Directions

My Pet Cat

1. Trace and cut out a gray head.
2. Trace and cut out a gray body.
3. Glue the cat together on blue paper.
4. Draw a face.
5. Trace and cut out an orange bowl.
6. Glue the bowl next to the cat.
7. Write the cat's name on the bowl.

Follow-the-Directions Pocket Chart Activities Scholastic Teaching Resources

Getting Started

This project is a nice way to celebrate Be Kind to Animals Week, during the first week of May. To begin, ask students which animal they prefer, dogs or cats. Take a vote and then chart the results. Make a K-W-L chart about cats (What I Know, What I Want to Know, What I Learned). Read some nonfiction books about cats together, such as *Cats* by Gail Gibbons (Holiday House, 1998). Then complete the chart with information students discovered about cats.

Variations & Extensions

✳ Allow students to choose the color of their cat and its bowl. Provide construction paper in various colors, and modify the pocket chart instructions as follows:
  1. Choose a color for your cat.
  2. Trace and cut out the cat's head and body.
  3. Glue the cat together on a sheet of paper.
  4. Draw a face.
  5. Choose a color for the cat's bowl.
  6. Trace and cut out the bowl.
  7. Glue the bowl next to the cat.
  8. Write the cat's name on the bowl.

✳ Ask students to write or dictate a story about an adventure on which their new pet embarks. Have them add an illustration of their favorite part.

✳ Explain that not all cats make good pets. Ask students what types of cats fall under this category, such as lions, tigers, cheetahs, and bobcats. Explain that these cats are found in the wild. Research wild cats. Talk about the similarities and differences between wild and domestic cats. Use a Venn diagram to chart the information.

✳ As a group or individual activity, think of adjectives that describe the cat in the completed project. Write these on self-sticking notes and stick them around the project. If you have completed the puppy project (pages 36–37), do the same for the completed puppy. Compare the adjectives students used. Did they use any of the same words for both cats and dogs? Students can use these adjectives as a starting place for writing or dictating poems about a cat and a dog.

Book Links

Cats
by Gail Gibbons
(Holiday House, 1998)

Henry and Mudge and the Happy Cat
by Cynthia Rylant
(Simon & Schuster, 1990)

Mr. Putter and Tabby Pour the Tea
by Cynthia Rylant
(Harcourt, 1994)

Mrs. Katz and Tush
by Patricia Polacco
(Bantam, 1992)

Pet Show!
by Ezra Jack Keats
(Macmillan, 1972)

Pet Wash
by Dayle Ann Dodds
(Candlewick, 2001)

Growing Flowers

Themes & Concepts

- flowers • plants • seasons
- colors • heights

Materials

- ✔ 7 sentence strips
- ✔ flower and flowerpot templates (page 74)
- ✔ 9- by 12-inch brown, red, blue, and yellow construction paper
- ✔ 12- by 18-inch light blue construction paper
- ✔ pencils
- ✔ scissors
- ✔ glue
- ✔ green markers or crayons

Pocket Chart Directions

Growing Flowers

1. Trace and cut out three brown flowerpots.
2. Trace and cut out one red flower.
3. Trace and cut out one blue flower.
4. Trace and cut out one yellow flower.
5. Glue the flowerpots and flowers onto blue paper.
6. Draw stems and leaves.

Follow-the-Directions Pocket Chart Activities Scholastic Teaching Resources

Getting Started

Show children objects that are different heights. Discuss why objects are the heights they are—for example, why a chair seat needs to be lower than a table. Ask children to compare the heights of different things outside, such as trees and flowers.

When you model the project, show children how to place the first flower close to the flowerpot, the second flower a little farther away, and the third flower even farther away. Show children how to connect the flowers to the pots by drawing stems. Remind them to add leaves. Explain that their completed project does not need to look exactly like the sample.

Variations & Extensions

✳ Simplify the directions by making all of the flowers the same color. Change step 2 to read "Trace and cut out three [color] flowers" and then eliminate steps 3 and 4.

✳ Another way to simplify the project is to have children create only one flower. Then display the finished projects and discuss the differences in height of each student's flower.

✳ Invite children to write three-word messages on their flowerpots (one word per pot) such as, " I love you!" or "You're my friend." This makes a nice gift for a friend or family member.

✳ Give students practice following oral directions with this short extension activity. Ask students to look at their completed projects. Explain that you will ask them questions about their projects, but they should not answer you in words. Instead, they should listen to the directions and follow them to let you know their answer. Repeat the questions and directions if necessary. Here are some examples:
- Which of your flowers is the tallest? If your tallest flower is red, stand up and balance on one foot.
- Which of your flowers is the shortest? If your shortest flower is blue, wiggle your nose.
- Count your leaves. If you have fewer than three flowers, raise your arms. If you have more than three flowers, move your head from side to side.

Book Links

Bumblebee, Bumblebee, Do You Know Me?
by Anne Rockwell
(HarperCollins, 1999)

Flower Garden
by Eve Bunting
(Harcourt, 1994)

Jack's Garden
by Henry Cole
(Greenwillow, 1997)

Moo to You!

Themes & Concepts

- farms • cows

Materials

- ✔ 7 sentence strips
- ✔ cow body, head, and tail templates (pages 75–76)
- ✔ 9- by 12-inch white and black construction paper
- ✔ pencils
- ✔ scissors
- ✔ glue
- ✔ markers or crayons

Pocket Chart Directions

Moo to You!

1. Trace and cut out a white body.
2. Trace and cut out a white head.
3. Trace and cut out a black tail.
4. Cut out black spots.
5. Glue the cow together.
6. Draw a face.

Getting Started

Talk about what kinds of animals live on a farm. Show photographs or realistic illustrations of farm animals, including different kinds of cows. Ask students, "What are the characteristics of a cow? Are all cows the same color(s)?" Ask the students if they know where milk comes from. Read aloud a book that describes what happens on a dairy farm, such as *The Milk Makers* by Gail Gibbons (Aladdin Library, 1987) or *Milk: From Cow to Carton* by Aliki (HarperCollins, 1992). Together, make a chart of the process to show what students learned.

Variations & Extensions

* Sing, chant, or recite songs and poems that feature cows. Some favorites include "Hey, Diddle Diddle" and "Old MacDonald." Read aloud *And the Dish Ran Away With the Spoon* by Janet Stevens (Harcourt, 2001).

* Ask the class: "What's your favorite kind of milk? Is it chocolate milk? Strawberry? Skim?" Take a class survey and chart the results together. Add a title "Who-o-o-o Likes Milk?"

* To create a whole field of cows, display these projects on a bulletin board covered in green paper. Add a red paper barn and a farmer to complete the display.

* Read aloud fiction and nonfiction books about cows and farms, such as *Barn Dance!* by Bill Martin Jr. and John Archambault (Henry Holt, 1986) and *Farming* by Gail Gibbons (Holiday House, 1990). Compare and contrast these books. Discuss the features of fiction and nonfiction. Have students write their own collaborative books about farms. Create one book of fictional writing about farms and another book of facts about farms. To extend this activity, compare and contrast fiction and nonfiction books about other topics.

* Have students think of simple directions for drawing a cow (or another animal). You might base the drawing directions on the pocket chart directions on page 42. Write the directions together on chart paper. Then have children follow them to draw their own cows. For step-by-step directions to draw various animals and other pictures, refer to a drawing book such as *Follow the Directions and Draw It All by Yourself!* by Kristin Geller (Scholastic, 2001).

Book Links

Click Clack Moo: Cows That Type
by Doreen Cronin (Simon & Schuster, 2000)

Cow
by Jules Older (Charlesbridge, 1998)

Cows Can't Fly
by David Milgrim (Viking, 1998)

The Cow Who Wouldn't Come Down
by Paul Brett Johnson (Orchard, 1993)

There's Nothing to D-o-o-o!
by Judith Mathews (Browndeer, 1999)

Teddy Bear

Themes & Concepts

- bears
- comparing and contrasting

Materials

- ✔ 7 sentence strips
- ✔ teddy bear head, body, leg, and arm templates (page 77)
- ✔ 9- by 12-inch brown construction paper
- ✔ pencils
- ✔ scissors
- ✔ buttons
- ✔ glue
- ✔ markers or crayons

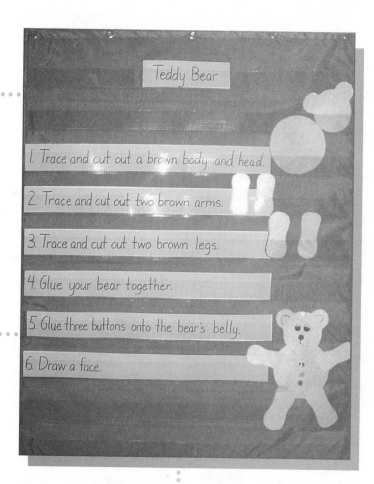

Pocket Chart Directions

Teddy Bear

1. Trace and cut out a brown body and head.
2. Trace and cut out two brown arms.
3. Trace and cut out two brown legs.
4. Glue your bear together.
5. Glue three buttons onto the bear's belly.
6. Draw a face.

Getting Started

Introduce this teddy bear project with this favorite rhyme:

Teddy bear, teddy bear, turn around.
Teddy bear, teddy bear, touch the ground.
Teddy bear, teddy bear, reach up high.
Teddy bear, teddy bear, touch the sky!

Have children do the motions as you chant the song together. Or, have students bring in bears and move them around as they recite the rhyme.

Variations & Extensions

✱ Extend the teddy bear song (see Getting Started) to reinforce following directions. Have children take turns making up verses while the rest of the class listens and follows the directions. Can students think of other songs that involve following directions? ("Hokey Pokey," "If You're Happy and You Know It," and so on) Sing these songs and add verses for additional practice with following directions.

✱ Have children create paper clothes for their bears. Students can cut out paper shirts, pants, hats, and so on from colored construction paper or patterned wrapping paper. Encourage them to add details with markers or crayons and then glue the clothes to their completed project.

✱ As a class, plan a teddy bear picnic. Invite students to bring a favorite stuffed friend from home. (Have extra stuffed animals on hand in case students are not able to bring in a toy from home.) Display the completed projects and read aloud one or more teddy bear stories (see Book Links).

✱ Read aloud *The Legend of the Teddy Bear* by Frank Murphy (Sleeping Bear Press, 2000). This book expands upon how the teddy bear was named after President Theodore Roosevelt.

✱ Research and discuss different kinds of bears, such as polar bears, grizzly bears, panda bears, and so on (see Book Links). As a group, list similarities and differences in size, color of fur, eating habits, homes, and so on.

✱ Ask students how they might create a paper panda bear instead of a teddy bear. Work together to write simple cut-and-paste directions on chart paper. Then provide black and white construction paper and other supplies and have children follow the directions.

Book Links

Grizzly Bears
by Gail Gibbons
(Holiday House, 2003)

Growl! A Book About Bears
by Melvin Berger
(Cartwheel, 1999)

Polar Bears
by Gail Gibbons
(Holiday House, 2002)

The Teddy Bear
by David McPhail
(Henry Holt, 2002)

The Teddy Bears' Picnic
by Jimmy Kennedy
(HarperCollins, 1996)

Up Bear, Down Bear
by Trudy Harris
(Houghton Mifflin, 2001)

Shape Robot

Themes & Concepts

- shapes • colors • robots

Materials

✔ 7 sentence strips
✔ shape templates (pages 78–80)
✔ blue, red, and yellow construction paper
✔ pencils
✔ scissors
✔ glue

Pocket Chart Directions

Shape Robot

1. Trace and cut out a large blue square.
2. Trace and cut out a large red rectangle.
3. Trace and cut out two long yellow rectangles.
4. Trace and cut out two small yellow rectangles.
5. Trace and cut out different shapes for details.
6. Glue your robot together.

Getting Started

Invite children to share what they know about robots. Explain that robots are made of different mechanical parts. Describe some parts a robot may have and show pictures of various mechanical parts. Ask students to identify the shapes they see. Can they find similar shapes in the classroom?

Explain to students that the details on their robots do not need to look like the sample project. Encourage them to create their own unique design.

Variations & Extensions

❋ Provide precut smaller shapes for step 5. Change the directions for the last two steps as follows:
   5. Glue your robot together.
   6. Glue different shapes for details.

❋ Provide markers and crayons. Add the following step:
   7. Draw details on your robot.

❋ Before students glue the parts together, show them how to fold the robot's arms back and forth accordion-style.

❋ Stock your arts and crafts center with small boxes, empty toilet tissue rolls, precut paper or cardboard shapes, pipe cleaners, empty thread spools, buttons, and so on. Invite students to use these materials to create their own three-dimensional robots.

❋ Use this activity in conjunction with the Teddy Bear activity (pages 44–45) to create projects for a holiday toy display.

❋ Using the templates from this activity as well as templates for additional shapes, have children create simple pictures out of shapes. Then have students write or dictate directions for creating these pictures. Students can then trade sets of directions and create each other's projects.

❋ Challenge students to use their imaginations and program their robots. What directions would they give their robots to follow? Children might come up with instructions such as "Follow me wherever I go," "Tie my shoes when they are untied," or "Help me with my homework."

Book Links

Color Zoo
by Lois Ehlert
(HarperCollins, 1989)

Rolie Polie Olie
by William Joyce
(HarperCollins, 1999)

Sammy and the Robots
by Ian Whybrow
(Orchard, 2001)

The Shape of Things
by Dayle Ann Dodds
(Candlewick, 1994)

Shape Space
by Cathryn Falwell
(Beacon, 1992)

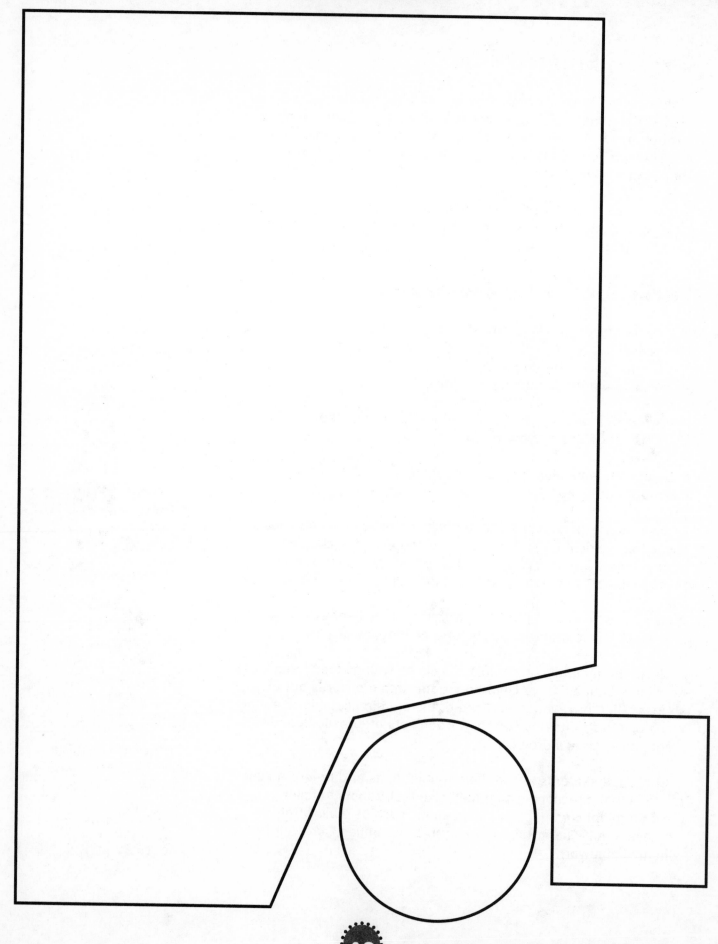

Follow-the-Directions Pocket Chart Activities Scholastic Teaching Resources

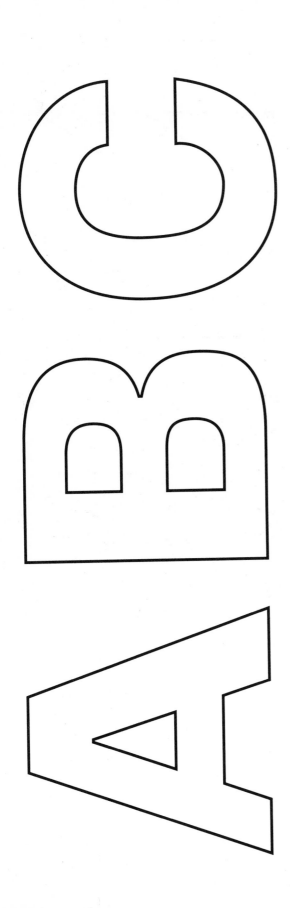

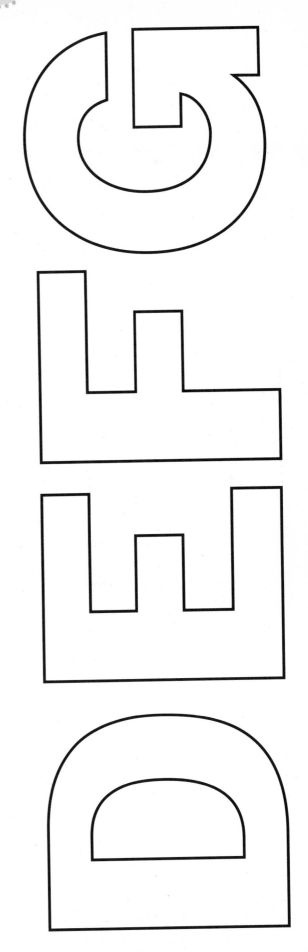

Follow-the-Directions Pocket Chart Activities Scholastic Teaching Resources

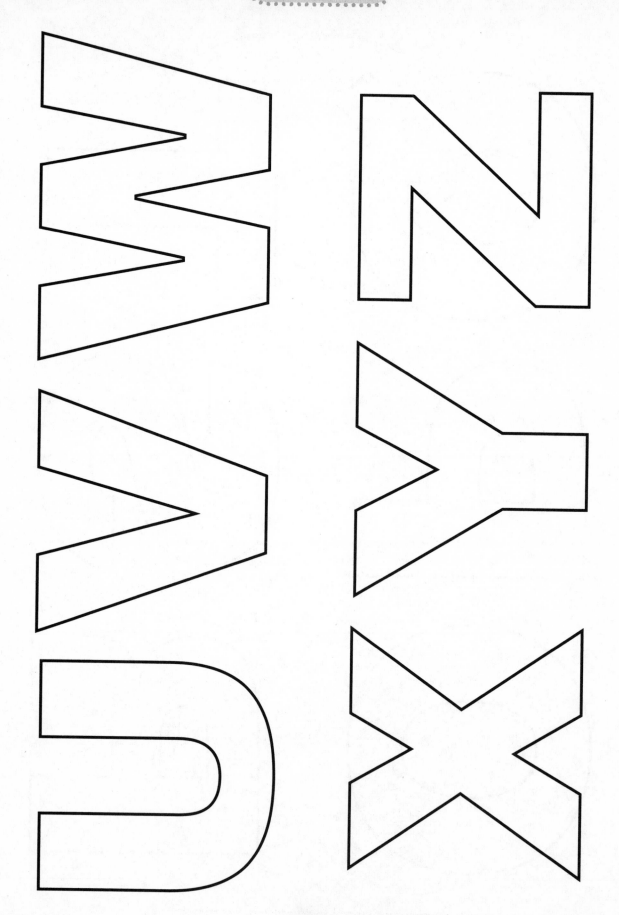

Follow-the-Directions Pocket Chart Activities Scholastic Teaching Resources

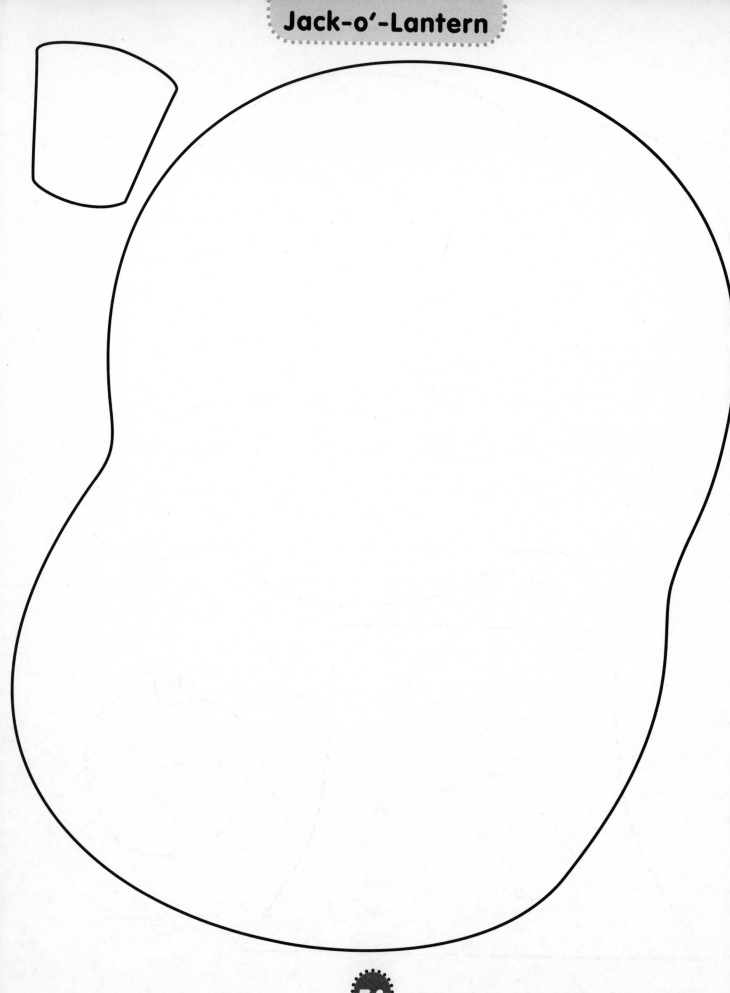

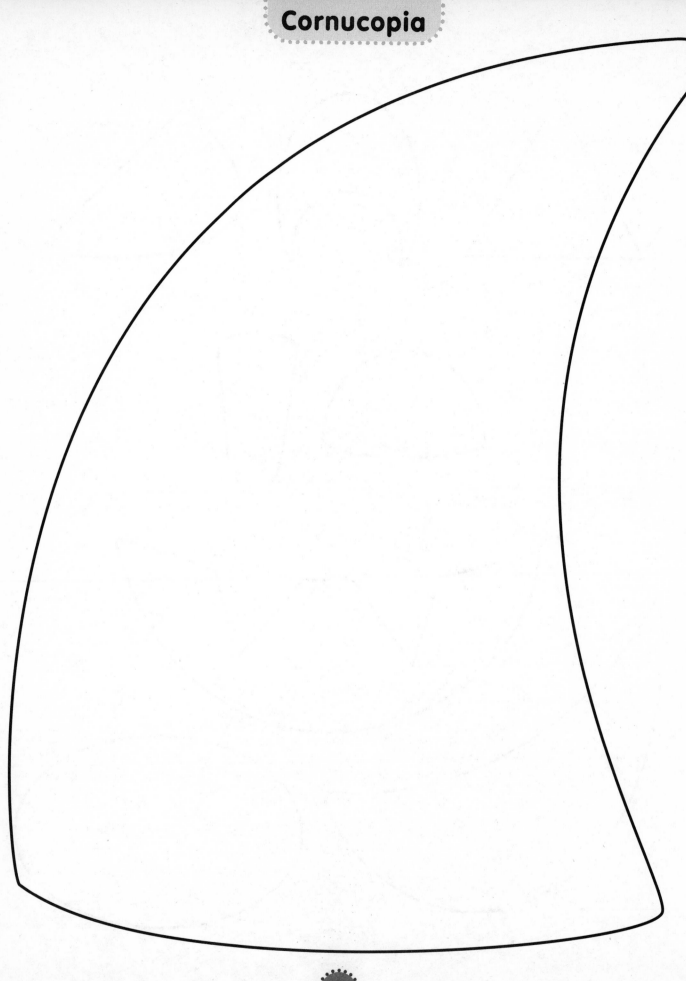

Cornucopia

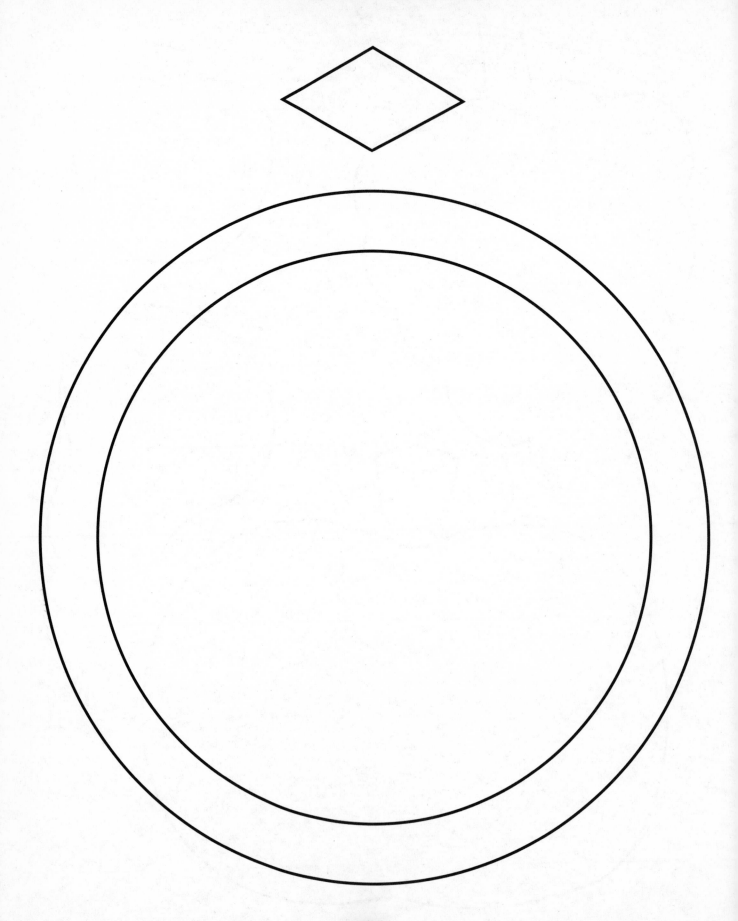

Follow-the-Directions Pocket Chart Activities Scholastic Teaching Resources

Make Your Own Sundae

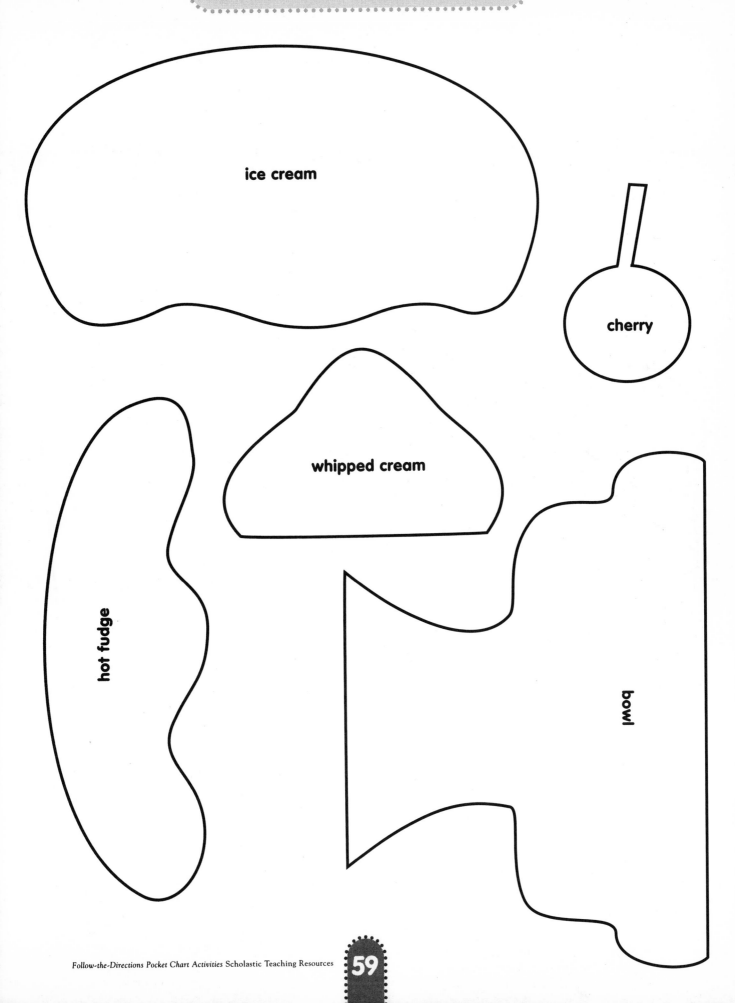

ice cream

cherry

whipped cream

hot fudge

bowl

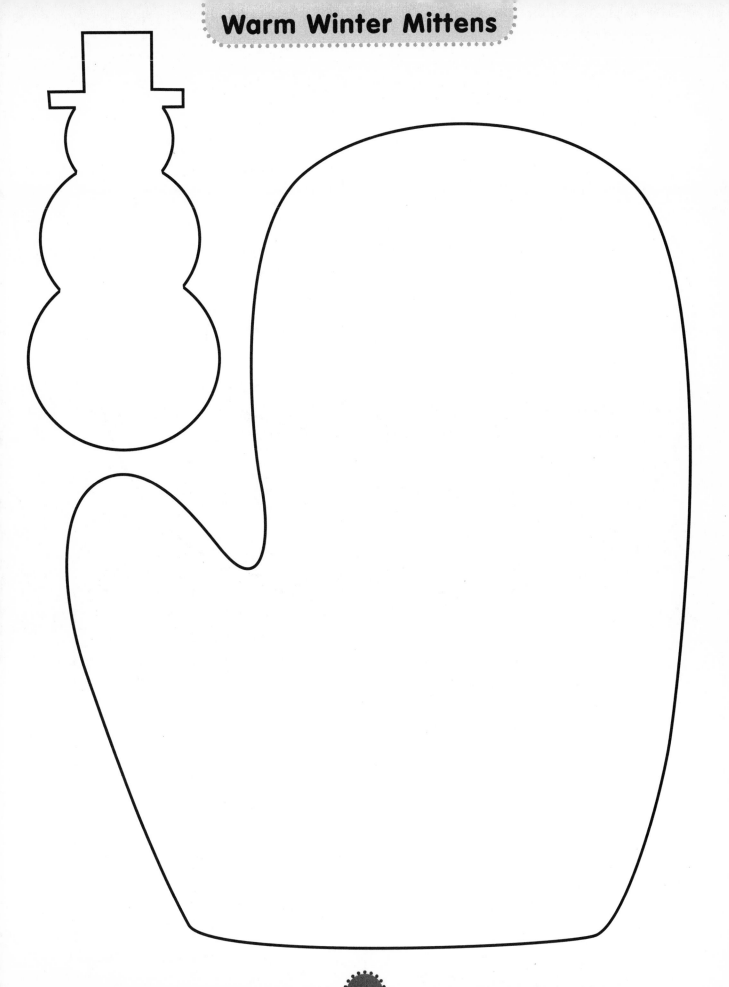

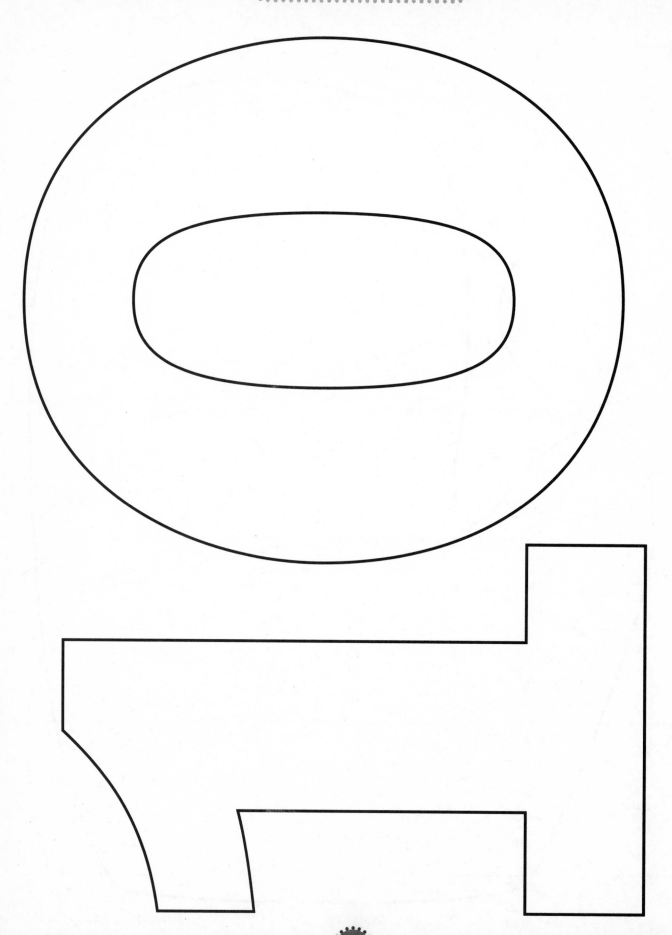

Follow-the-Directions Pocket Chart Activities Scholastic Teaching Resources

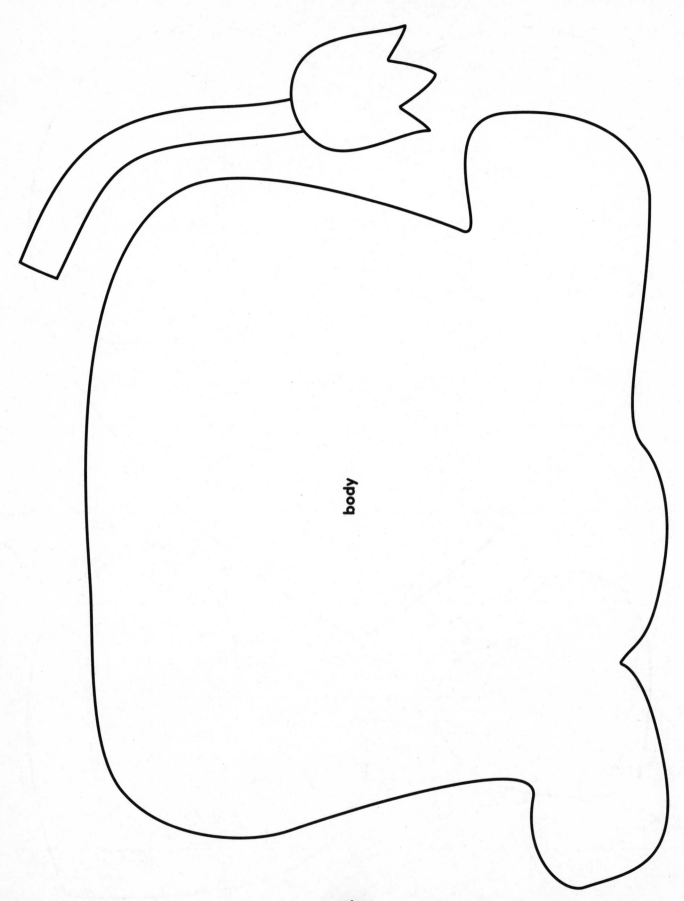

body

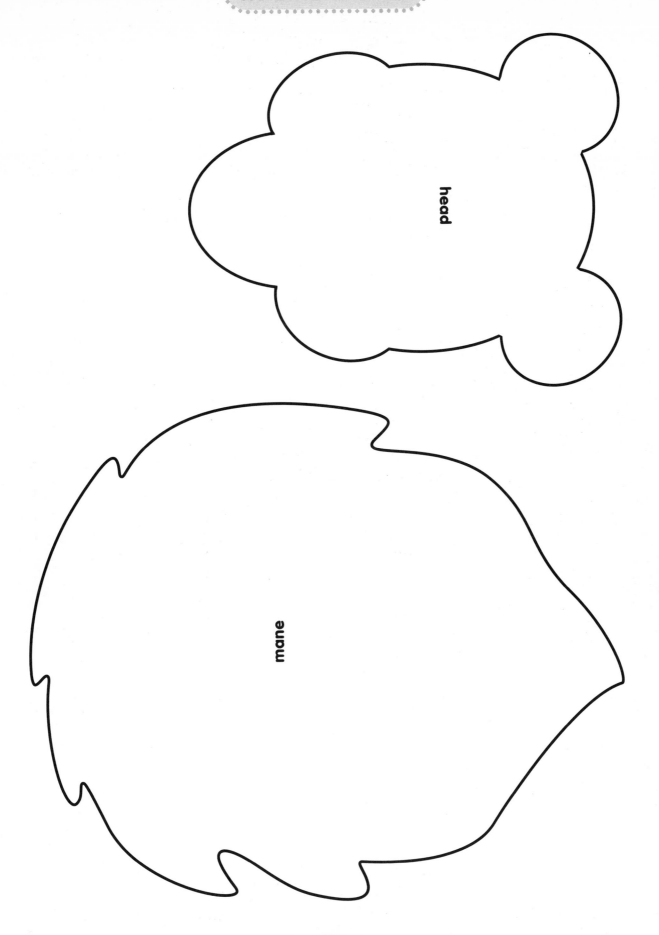

head

mane

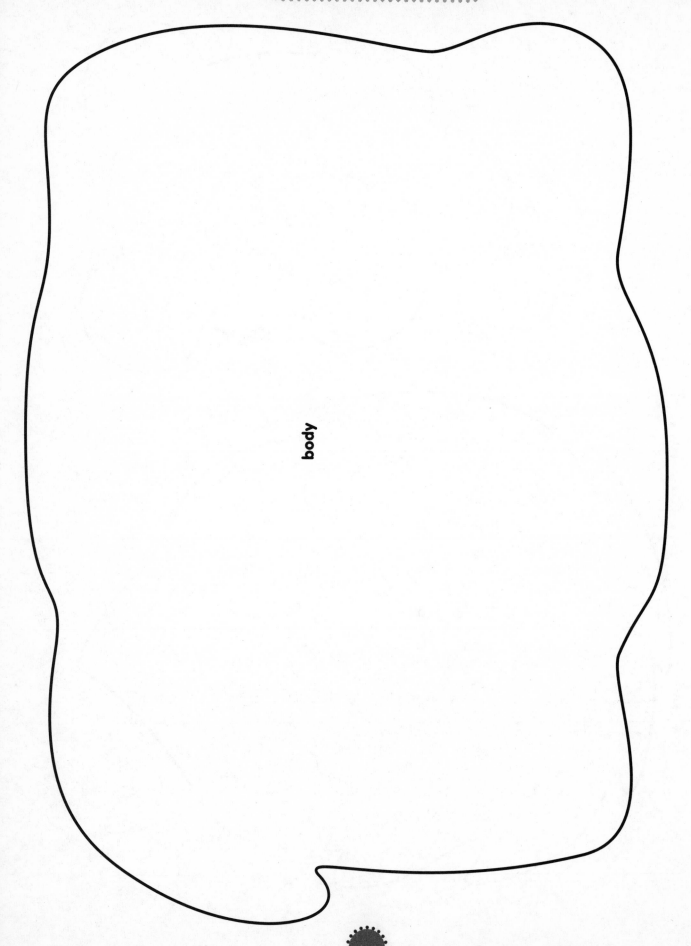

body

Follow-the-Directions Pocket Chart Activities Scholastic Teaching Resources

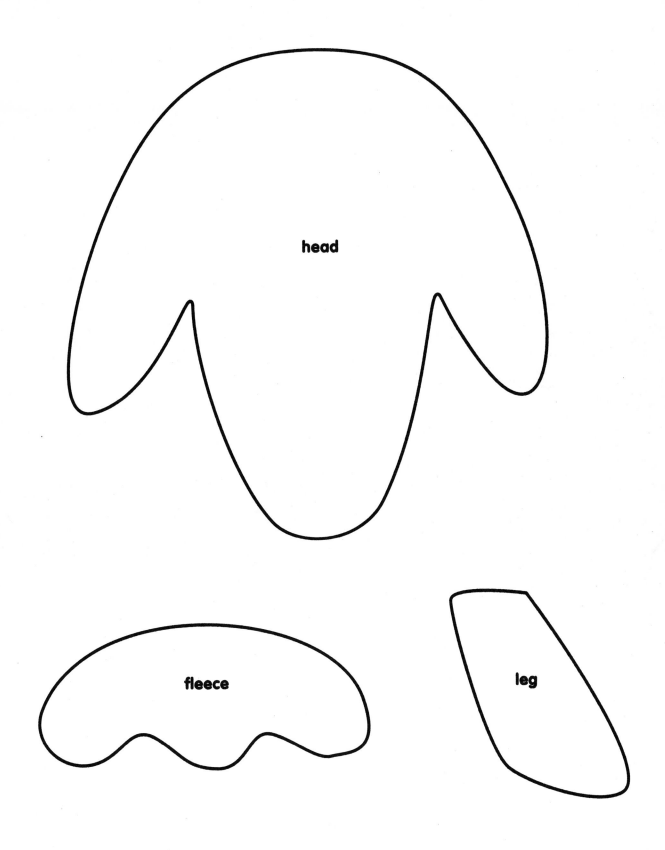

head

fleece

leg

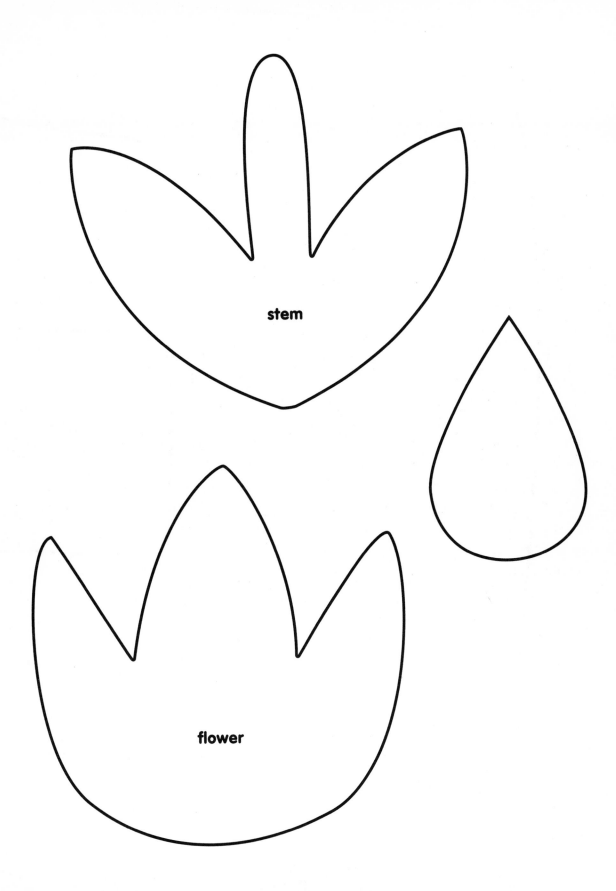

stem

flower

My Pet Puppy

Follow-the-Directions Pocket Chart Activities Scholastic Teaching Resources

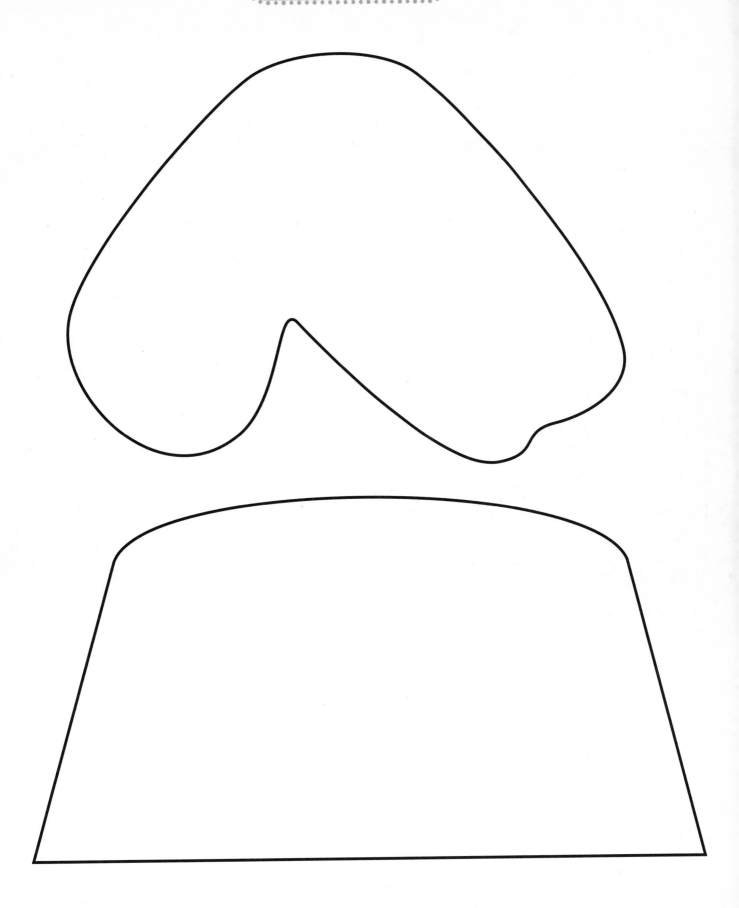

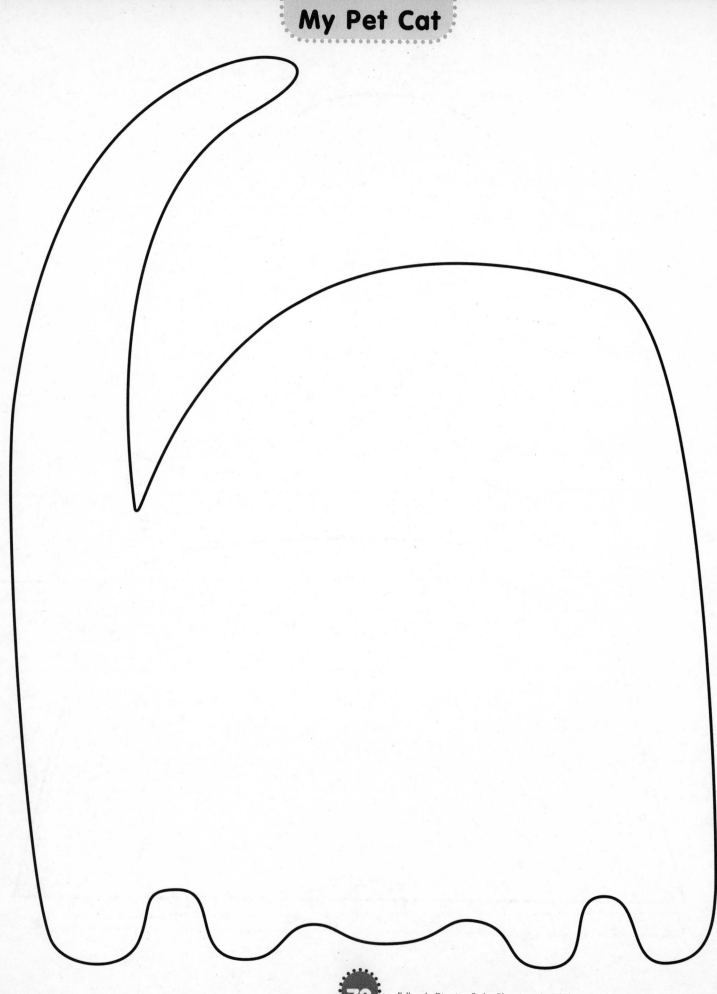

My Pet Cat

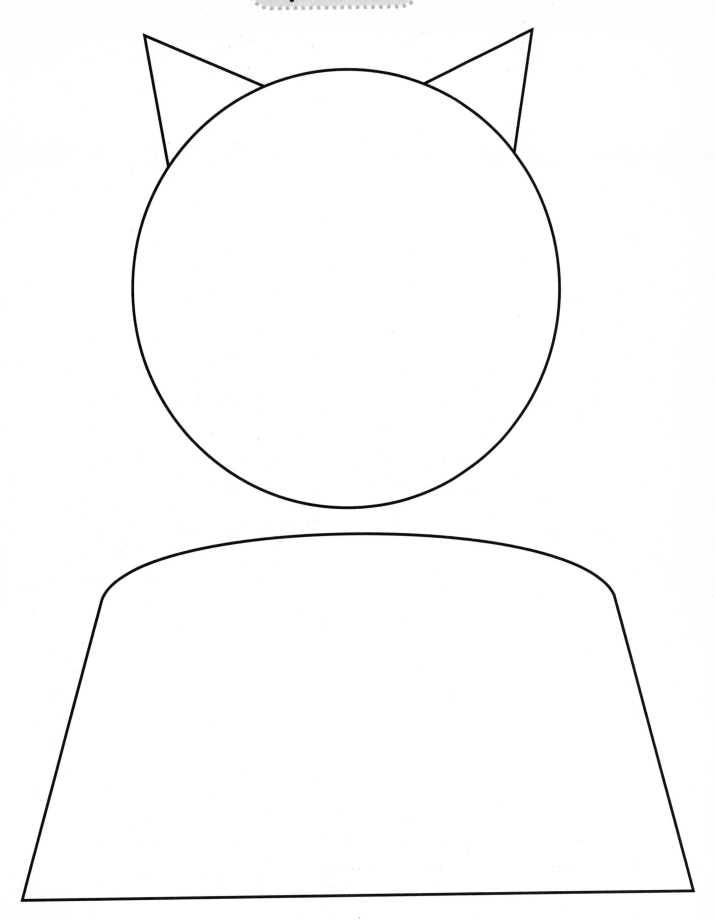

Follow-the-Directions Pocket Chart Activities Scholastic Teaching Resources

Moo to You!

Follow-the-Directions Pocket Chart Activities Scholastic Teaching Resources

Teddy Bear

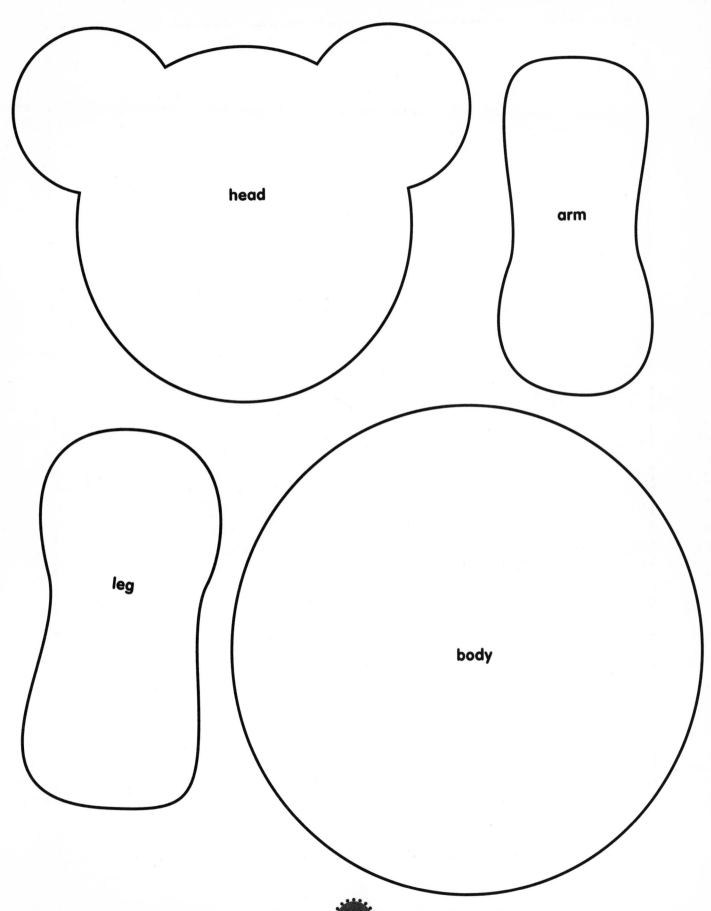

head

arm

leg

body

body

head

arm

leg

Shapes for Details